DEVELOPING A POSITIVE ATTITUDE IN LIFE

And she said, Let thine handmaid find grace in thy sight. So the woman went her way, and did eat, and her countenance was no more sad.

1 Samuel 1:18

by

Franklin N. Abazie

Developing A Positive Attitude In Life
COPYRIGHT@ 2017 BY Franklin N Abazie
ISBN: 978-1-94513303-9

All right reserved. This book or any portion thereof may not be reproduced or used in any manner whatsoever without the express written permission of the publisher, except for the use of brief quotations in a book review. All Bible quotes are from King James Version and others as noted.

Published by: F N ABAZIE PUBLISHING HOUSE- aka, Empowerment Bookstore.

That I may publish with the voice of thanksgiving and tell of all thy wondrous works.
Psalms 26:7

To order additional copies, wholesales
or booking:
Call the Church office (973-372-7518),
or Empowerment Bookstore Hotline (973-393-8518)

Worship address:
343 Sanford Avenue Newark New Jersey 07106
Administrative Head Office address:
33 Schley Street Newark New Jersey 07112
Email:pastorfranknto@yahoo.com
Website www.fnabaziehealingministries.org
Publishing House: www.fnabaziepublishinghouse.org

This book is a production of F N Abazie Publishing House.
A publication Arms of Miracle of God Ministries 2017.
First Edition

CONTENTS

THE MANDATE OF THE COMMISSION iv
ARMS OF THE COMMISSION v
INTRODUCTION vi
CHAPTER 1
1 The Lifestyle of Joy 1
CHAPTER 2
2 How To Remain Positive In Life 8
CHAPTER 3
3 Prayer of Salvation 45
CHAPTER 4
4 About The Author 57

THE MANDATE OF THE COMMISSION

"The moment is due to impact your world through the revival of the healing & miracle ministry of Jesus Christ of Nazareth."

"I am sending you to restore health unto thee and I will heal thee of thy wounds, said the Lord of Host."

ARMS OF THE COMMISSION

1) F N Abazie Ministries-Miracle of God Ministries (Miracle Chapel Intl)

2) F N Abazie TV Ministries: Global Television Ministry Outreach

3) F N Abazie Radio Ministries: Radio Broadcasting Outreach

4) F N Abazie Publishing House: Book Publication

5) F N Abazie Bible School: also called Word of Healing Bible School (W.O.H.B.S)

6) F N Abazie Evangelistic Ass: Miracle of God Ministries: Global Crusade

7) Empowerment Bookstore: Book distribution

8) F N Abazie Helping Hands: Meeting the help of the needy world wide

9) F N Abazie Disaster Recovery Mission: Global Disaster Recovery

10) F N Abazie Prison Ministry: Prison Ministry for all convicts "Second chance"

Some of our ministry arms are waiting the appointed time to commence.

FAVOR CONFESSION

Father thank you for making me righteous and accepted through the blood of Jesus Christ. Because of that, I am blessed and highly favored by God. I am the subject of your affection. Your favor surrounds me as a shield, and the first thing that people see around me is your favored shield.

Thank you that I have favor with you and man today. All day long people go out of their way to bless me and help me. I have favor with everyone that I deal with today. Doors that were once closed are now opened for me. I receive preferential treatment, and I have special privileges, I am Gods favored child.

No good thing will he withhold from me. Because of Gods favor my enemies cannot triumph over my life. I have supernatural increase and promotion. I declare restoration to everything that the devil has stolen from my life. I have honor in the midst of my adversaries and an increase in assets, especially in real estate and expansion of territories.

Because I am highly favored by God, I experience great victories, supernatural turnarounds, and miraculous breakthrough in the midst of great impossibilities. I receive recognition, prominence, and honor. Petitions are granted to me even by ungodly authorities. Policies, rules, regulations, and laws are changed and reverse on my behalf.

I win battles that I don't even have to fight, because God fights them for me. This is the day, the set time and the designated moment for me to experience the free favor of God, that profusely and lavishly abound on my behalf in Jesus name. **Amen.**

INTRODUCTION

"And she said, Let thine handmaid find grace in thy sight. So the woman went her way, and did eat, and her countenance was no more sad." **1 Samuel 1:18**

Positive attitude is all it takes for a change of destiny in life. If I may put it this way, "An attitude of gratitude will change our altitude in life." From the opening scripture above, once Hannah changed her attitude she secured her miracle baby. It is written, "And she said, Let thine handmaid find grace in thy sight. So the woman went her way, and did eat, and her countenance was no more sad." **(1 Samuel 1:18)**

Every great destiny is built from the mystery of a positive attitude in life. In this publication, you will appreciate the mystery behind positive attitude in life. As you remain optimistic concerning your future, every prevailing challenges in your life will be subdued by the power of God.

In this book I have tried to bring to light some strong mysteries about maintaining continual joy, and praise as a lifestyle. Unless you remain calm and optimistic in the midst of prevailing challenges, we will miss our glorious future. There is absolute power in positive people who believe and hope in God.

"For to him that is joined to all the living there is hope: for a living dog is better than a dead lion."
Ecclesiastes 9:4

Unless we change our mentality in life, we shall forever remain in want. Unless we embrace positive thinking in life, we shall forever remain failures in life. This publication is about positive thinking, it encourages pessimistic people to change the way they think and reflect on prevailing challenges in life. I see you changing your mentality as you embrace the teachings in this book. A positive attitude is all it takes for a successful living.Unless there is a change of heart we cannot secure a change of destiny in life.

In my own opinion, your mentality determines the outcome of your life. For we will never win, unless we think like winners in life. *I pray you change your attitude and embrace the laws of God into your life in Jesus Name. I pray, receive the winners mentality in Jesus Name. Amen*

HIS DESTINY WAS THE **CROSS**....

HIS PURPOSE WAS **LOVE**.....

HIS REASON WAS **YOU**....

And she said, Let thine handmaid find grace in thy sight. So the woman went her way, and did eat, and her countenance was no more sad.

1 Samuel 1:18

PRAYER POINT OF ENCOURAGEMENT

"If ye shall ask any thing in my name, I will do it.."
John 14:14

I cover my body with the blood of Jesus, in the name of Jesus.

I plead the blood of Jesus over my family.

I reject every demonic interruption against my life in the name of Jesus.

Arise Lord God, open the gates of prosperity in the name of Jesus.

Fire of God, melt all witchcraft covens away like wax with your fire, in the name of Jesus.

Fire of God visit all witchcraft incantations with thunder, earthquake, and great noise, in the name of Jesus.

O God arise and instruct your angels to send unquenchable fire upon witchcraft habitation and shrine, in the name of Jesus.

Angels of God arise and slay the power of the wicked, in the name of Jesus.

Gates of Heaven refuse to carry out the instruction of witchdoctors assigned against me in the name of Jesus.

I deprogram and cancel all witchcraft prophecies by the power in the blood of Jesus, in the name of Jesus.

I decree judgment on witchcraft into the heavens, in the name of Jesus.

Fire of God, arise, and cast abominable things upon witchcraft, in the name of Jesus.

Hand of God, let the table of witchcraft becomes their snare, in the name of Jesus.

Let the eyes of the witches assigned against me be darkened, in the name of Jesus.

Let their covens become desolate so that none can dwell in them, in the name of Jesus.

Pray this prayer three hot times: Let every witchcraft powers flying against me crash land and die, in the name of Jesus.

No witch or wizard shall prosper in my environment in the name of Jesus.

Water spirits that are networking with witchcraft against me, I judge you by fire, in the name of Jesus.

Queen of heaven that is networking with witchcraft against me, I judge you by fire, in the name of Jesus.

Let the sun go down on witchcraft networks in the name of Jesus.

Let the sun smite them by day and the moon by night, in the name of Jesus.

Let the stars in their curses fight against witches and wizards in the name of Jesus.

I shut down all witchcraft buildings with the key of David, in the name of Jesus.

Father God, arise and send out your whirlwind with great pain upon the head of witchcraft, in the name of Jesus.

O Lord, arise and trample down every witchcraft coven in the name of Jesus.

Father God, arise and cause stormy wind to fall upon witchcraft powers in the name of Jesus.

Father God, arise and bring the day of disaster upon the heads of witchcraft in the name of Jesus.

I come against all enchantment of witchcraft in the name of Jesus.

I destroy every agenda of witchcraft over my family I cut you off in the name of Jesus.

Witchcraft in the waters I crush you powers in the name of Jesus.

Witchcraft agenda for my destiny, roast by fire in the name of Jesus.

Every witchcraft power assigned to convert my life to a dustbin I dislodge you in the name of Jesus.

Witchcraft powers assigned to resurrect affliction in my life, die by fire in the name of Jesus.

Every witchcraft game plan over my success I destroy you, in the name of Jesus.

Every yoke manufactured by witchcraft to attack my life catch your owner in the name of Jesus.

Every pregnancy of sorrow assigned against my breakthrough by witchcraft powers I abort you now, in the name of Jesus.

I offset every witchcraft plan set up against my life, in the name of Jesus.

I break every witchcraft imprisonment over my life in the name of Jesus.

Every witchcraft remote control against my life I block you out in the name of Jesus.

Witchcraft powers sponsoring repeated problems in my life carry your problems in the name of Jesus.

I destroy every occultist man/woman assigned against me, in the name of Jesus.

Every household witchcraft assigned to waste my life be wasted in the name of Jesus.

Witchcraft altars and priests, die in the name of Jesus.

Every yoke designed by marine powers against my life, break in the name of Jesus.

Every evil load of witchcraft go back to your sender in the name of Jesus.

Every witchcraft prayer against my life scatter, in the name of Jesus.

Every environmental witchcraft be disgraced in the name of Jesus.

I destroy every witchcraft grip upon my family in the name of Jesus.

I shatter every witchcraft initiations against my destiny in the name of Jesus.

Satanic decree over my life I cancel you now in the name of Jesus.

Witchcraft manipulations of my finances die in the name of Jesus.

Every witchcraft padlock hanging against me lock your owner in the name of Jesus.

Every witchcraft engagement over my success break in the name of Jesus.

Every ancestral witchcraft claim over my life break in the name of Jesus.

I destroy the power of stagnation and limitation in the name of Jesus.

I cut down every tree of failure in my family line, in the name of Jesus.

I destroy every pin of witchcraft in my family line, in the name of Jesus.

Every witchcraft covenant working against my life be broken in Jesus name.

Every witchcraft register bearing my name catch fire in the name of Jesus.

Every witchcraft documents written against me be consumed by fire, in the name of Jesus.

Every witchcraft informant that is observing my destiny be paralyzed, in the name of Jesus.

Every image carved against me catch fire, in the name of Jesus.

Every witchcraft authority over my destiny break in the name of Jesus.

Every tree planted against my freedom catch fire in the name of Jesus.

Every satanic road block clear away by fire in the name of Jesus.

Every witchcraft concoction inside my body melt away by fire in the name of Jesus.

I destroy every Jezebel spirit, against my life, in the name of Jesus.

Father Lord arise in your anger and pursues my pursuer, in the name of Jesus.

Every foundation of witchcraft in my family catch fire, in the name of Jesus.

I pollute the food of witchcraft powers with the blood of Jesus in the name of Jesus.

Every seat of witchcraft working against me receive the fire of God in the name of Jesus.

Let their communication system be disrupted and be destroyed in the name of Jesus.

Let their throne be dismantled by fire and by thunder of God in the name of Jesus.

I set the fire of God into their place of refuge in the name of Jesus.

Let the east wind of God pull down the strong hold of stubborn witchcraft in the name of Jesus.

I disintegrate and scatter all the network of witchcraft in the name of Jesus.

Let the transportation of witchcraft power catch fire and burn to ashes in the name of Jesus.

Every hindering forces against my life receive double confusion in the name of Jesus.

Let the weapons of the enemy turn against them in the name of Jesus.

I speak confusion into the storehouses of witchcraft and I enter in and possess my possession in the name of Jesus.

Let their altars catch fire and burn to ashes in the name of Jesus.

I use the hammer of God to destroy their padlock in the name of Jesus.

Let the traps, nets and snares of the enemy catch them unawares in the name of Jesus.

Every demonic projection against my progress backfire in the name of Jesus.

Every witchcraft burial of my destiny receive fire and be exhumed in the name of Jesus.

Every bewitchment of my life receive the Holy Ghost fire in the name of Jesus.

I destroy every forces of hell hindering my breakthrough in the Name of Jesus.

Every power of witchcraft interrupting my life, receive the fire of the Lord, in the name of Jesus.

Lord God, destroy every satanic to forces, trouble my life in the name of Jesus.

Any powers drawing my blood vomit it and die in the name of Jesus.

Every power that has tasted my blood will not stop vomiting until it confesses in the name of Jesus.

Blood of Jesus cause confusion in the stomach of witchcraft in the name of Jesus.

Thou power of witchcraft monitor die in the name of Jesus.

Let the night birds of witchcraft be massacred by the angels of God in the name of Jesus.

Witchcraft from my place of birth militating against my life die in the name of Jesus.

Every witchcraft power, be destroyed in the name of Jesus.

I overthrow any kingdom of witchcraft assigned against my life in the name of Jesus.

Let the blood of Jesus destroy every witchcraft assigned against my life in the name of Jesus.

Every witchcraft exchange of my virtues be frustrated in the name of Jesus.

I destroy every coffin of witches plotted against my life, in the Name of Jesus.

Any witchcraft power projecting into the body of an animal in order to do me harm be trapped in that body forever, in the name of Jesus.

Let every witchcraft power be covered with shame in the name of Jesus.

Every chain of inherited witchcraft in my family break in the name of Jesus.

Every wisdom of witchcraft working against me be converted to madness in the name of Jesus.

I pray, Let the imagination of witchcraft against me be neutralized in the name of Jesus.

Father God let every witchcraft decision against my life be scattered in the name of Jesus.

O God smites witchcraft powers by their cheekbones in the name of Jesus.

Every witchcraft burial of my virtues I reverse you now in the name of Jesus.

Any tongue anointed by Satan against me catch fire in the name of Jesus.

HOW DO I DEVELOP A POSITIVE ATTITUDE IN LIFE?

----*Faith in God*

As long as we live, obstacles and trials will come our way. We must develop strong faith in God, and expect the best in life, at all times. Jesus said *"These things I have spoken unto you, that in me ye might have peace. In the world ye shall have tribulation: but be of good cheer; I have overcome the world."* (John 16:33)

Faith in God is all it takes to become an overcomer in life. Although the devil takes advantage of our fears in life, God works with our faith, for our deliverance, promotion, and victory in life. It is written *"For whatsoever is born of God overcometh the world: and this is the victory that overcometh the world, even our faith."* (1 John 5:4)

----*We must be optimistic*

We must always engage our mind to our heart desires. You cannot produce, or give what you do not have. Unless you think positively, you will never see positive result in life. We must therefore develop consciously positive mindset against every affair of our life. Listen to me, pessimistic people cannot go far in life.

For us to succeed in any area of our life, we must expect the best out of every odd situation. We must always expect the best result from the worst. We are admonished by the bible, to never expect the failure or the worst from any prevailing circumstance. As believers, it is scriptural to be optimistic in life. It is written *"Who is he that overcometh the world, but he that believeth that Jesus is the Son of God"* (1 John 5:5)

CHAPTER 1
THE LIFESTYLE OF JOY

"…..neither be ye sorry; for the joy of the Lord is your strength." Neh 8:10

Joy is a mystery of life that has power to exempt us- believers from the horrors of life. Unless we cultivate and maintain the spirit of joy in our lives, we shall forever remain disappointed and in despair in life. The cheapest way to overcome, and subdue prevailing obstacles in life is by embracing *the Joy of the Lord* in our life.

One great man of God was asked one time, "*Have you ever experienced obstacles in life?*" He said "*May be it came, and I didn't know.*" This great man of God, is a renowned man of joy and of faith in life. Every time we worry and complain in life, we make ourselves vulnerable to the assault of the devil.

One man once said and I quote *"when you are depressed, you are living in the past, when you are anxious, you are living in the future, but when you are at peace, you are living in the present".*

We must always realize that nothings comes free in life. As free as "Salvation" is to us, Jesus paid the price for it on the cross. The good news is that, no matter what comes our way in life - whether it's personal hardship or maybe just the roller coaster of life, when we experience good times with families, or frustrating difficult times in life- through it all, we have a relationship with our God. God is our very present help in the day of trouble-who's Joy is our strength. *"....yet believing, ye rejoice with joy unspeakable and full of glory."* **(1 Peter 1:8)**

----Life can be tough: Don't give up

As long as you can learn to be content in life, make yourself happy regardless of the odd, you shall surely prevail against the will of the enemy in life. One of the greatest mystery of *"the Joy of the Lord"* is to understand that *"nothing last forever in life"*. Often during frustrating, and challenging moments, we tend to forget that "nothing last forever." Every challenge has an expiration date. As long as there is a beginning, it shall surely come to an end.

It is written *"For his anger endureth but a moment; in his favour is life: weeping may endure for a night, but joy cometh in the morning."* (Psalm 30:5). It takes the Joy of the Lord to understand that regardless of the prevailing trials, and struggles against your life, it shall surely come to an end someday. It is written *"For our light affliction, which is but for a moment, worketh for us a far more exceeding and eternal weight of glory;"* (2 Cor 4:17)

The race of Life can be tough, but as believers, we must not give up in life. We are told that only those that endue to the end shall be saved. It is written *"And ye shall be hated of all men for my name's sake: but he that endureth to the end shall be saved."* (Matthew 10:22) It takes the *"Joy of the Lord"* to keep living a victorious life. You may not have the money to pay your next rent or

Chapter 1   The Lifestyle of Joy

your next telephone bill, do not give up. Perhaps you are unemployed, do not give up. May be you are experiencing hardship in your relationship, do not give up. God has a plan of good and not evil, to give you an expected end and a future.

Joy and happiness are often misunderstood to be the same thing, the truth is that, they are very different. Happiness is an emotion that is aroused in us when we buy a new thing, or get a promotion at work.

Although, happiness in life depend on the present change of circumstance with conditions attached to it. Joy is an emotion that occurs within us when we develop an attitude of genuine gratefulness, thankfulness for life, for our relationships families and with others, keeping hope and faith alive *that with God all things are possible in life.* There is a great difference between joy and happiness in life. Often most of us are happy every time we experience a good outcome in life. But a good outcome is not guaranteed in life every time.

For the most part, most of us live in denial in life. We must embrace the *Joy of the Lord* if we must be realistic about our lives. Happiness is not an emotion that we learn; we inevitable become happy every time we see our heart desire come to pass. But the *Joy of the Lord* is a spirit that dwell permanently in us, and rule our daily lives. Every man of faith is a man of joy. For faith worketh by love. The *Joy of the Lord* is powerful that it converts threats to opportunities, weaknesses into strength for every one that genuinely believes in God. It is written *"...but the righteous are bold as a lion."* (Proverb 28:1)

----Embrace the Joy of the Lord as a lifestyle

The Joy of the Lord is the source of good health in life. *"A merry heart doeth good like a medicine: but a broken spirit drieth the bones."* (Proverb 17:22) We are also told that *"The spirit of a man will sustain his infirmity; but a wounded spirit who can bear?"* (Proverb 18:14)

If you check out most sick people, they lack *"the Joy of the Lord."* Sickness and disease afflicts anyone who constantly murmur and complain about everything in life. Every time we lack the *Joy of the Lord* in our life, we let *fear, anger,* and *sadness* to afflict us with sickness. These three emotions if experienced in a prolonged state cause's sickness like high blood pressure, joint pains, liver palpitation, and headaches. etc.

Contrary to the Joy of the Lord, contentment, and happiness. These positive emotions are medicinal to the body. *"A merry heart doeth good like a medicine: but a broken spirit drieth the bones."* (Proverb 17:22) We must embrace the Joy of the Lord as a life style if we must experience long life. *"With long life will I satisfy him, and shew him my salvation"* (Psalms 91:16)

It is written *"I call heaven and earth to record this day against you, that I have set before you life and death, blessing and cursing: therefore choose life, that both thou and thy seed may live"* **(Deut 30:19)**

God gave us the option to live in *Joy, contentment, and happiness or in fear, anger, and sadness in life*. Irrespective of any prevailing circumstances confronting us in life. Some folks think that unless their prevailing circumstances changes, *fear, anger, and sadness* will not subside. Often we tend to forget that fear is false, evidence appearing real. Fear is more of an illusion than a reality. We have more probability of overcoming our fears, worries, and anxiety in life as believers.

What is fear?

F.........FALSE
E..................EXPERIENCE
A...................................APPEARING
R..REAL

F..................FACELESS
E.................................ENEMY
A..AFFLICTING
R...REASONING

F...........FREQUENTLY
E........................EXPECTED
A..ADVARSITY
R..REALIZED

F.................FANTACIZED
E.............................EXERGERATION
A..ABOVE
R..REALITY

F...... FIERCE
E...............EMOTION
A..............................AROUSING
R...RESTLESSNESS

F...........FACELESS
E......................EXPRESSION
A...ACKNOWLEDGED
R..REPEATEDLY

F...........FAILURE
E......................EXPECTED
A...AND
R..REHEARSED

Chapter 1   The Lifestyle of Joy

Unless we confront our anxiety, worries, and fear, we will never overcome the devil in life. *"There were they in great fear, where no fear was: for God hath scattered the bones of him that encampeth against thee: thou hast put them to shame, because God hath despised them"* (Psalms 53:5)

CHAPTER 2

HOW TO REMAIN POSITIVE IN LIFE

"For as he thinketh in his heart, so is he: Eat and drink, saith he to thee; but his heart is not with thee.
Proverb 23:7

It takes a change of heart for a change of attitude in life. Unless we change our heart positively, forever we will continue to experience failure in life. As Christians overcoming challenges, and conquering obstacles, is a validity of our faith in the Lord Jesus.

We must learn to cultivate that resilience by training our heart to remain positive when times are difficult. *"People tend to have a cognitive bias toward their failures, and toward negativity,"* says Matthew Della Porta, a positive psychologist and organizational consultant. Our brains are more likely to seek out negative information and store it more quickly to memory. *"These things I have spoken unto you, that in me ye might have peace. In the world ye shall have tribulation: but be of good cheer; I have overcome the world."* (John 16:33)

Most pessimistic people are trapped mentally by the negative thoughts they let envelop their heart. The act of acknowledging problems and confronting failures helps us succeed in life. But, whenever we try and fail, we must not blame ourselves for our failures in life. For us to overcome failure and negative outcome, we must focus on the positive in life.

HOW DO I REMAIN POSITIVE IN LIFE?

----Develop an attitude of gratitude.

Memories of failure in life and feeling of negative outcome has dominant power to glue into our memory. It is written *"In everything give thanks: for this is the will of God in Christ Jesus concerning you."* (1 Theo 5:18) We must learn to be grateful to God for the slightest accomplishment in our lives.

----Repeat positive affirmations.

Always say to yourself I will succeed against all odd. I am not a failure. I must make an impact in my life time. I am a Christian writer because that is how I see myself. Although I am not New York best seller author, but I am positive, and optimistic that very soon I will hit it in Jesus Mighty Name.

The act of repeating positive affirmation is faith in God in display. I have experienced a lot of financial challenges in ministry but I refused to quit. As a result of my positive attitude, I am not going to quit in my calling and assignment in life.

----Challenge negative thoughts.

"Whatever you do not confront has power to remain and to conquer." It takes action oriented faith to cast out negative thought. The devil uses negative thought

to distract us from our glorious future in life. It is written *"For I know the thoughts that I think toward you, saith the Lord, thoughts of peace, and not of evil, to give you an expected end."* (Jer 29:11)

I give you an example, if you start a business or a ministry and you experience frustration and financial difficulty to stay in business, you might say to yourself, "*I'm a failure."* That's not true in the spirit realm.

Temporary frustration does not mean *failure*. *"Winners do not quit in life and those who quit easily never win"*. Instead, interpret the same experience differently. You might say "*I did not plan ahead well that is why I experienced financial difficulty."* This interpretation is more proactive. "At first, this strategy will be hard and you'll think it doesn't work," But over time, it'll become automatic and negative thoughts will be less likely to dominate your heart. I pray you believe in God and become optimistic concerning the outcome of your glorious future in the Mighty Name of Jesus.

----*Faith*

It is written *"But without faith it is impossible to please him: for he that cometh to God must believe that he is, and that he is a rewarder of them that diligently seek him."* (Hebrew 11:6). Without faith in life we are heading into defeat in life. For us to remain positive in the midst of harsh economic predicament, we must develop faith in God and believe in ourselves in life. Most of us believers are not optimistic in life. To remain positive in life, we must optimistic in life. We must always see the positive out of any frustrating circumstances. *We must develop the positive vision in life, to see ahead, know ahead, and go ahead in life.*

---Good planning

One man said, if you fail to plan, you have planned to fail. We must always plan ahead in life as positive people. Men of impact are men that plan ahead. *"For which of you, intending to build a tower, sitteth not down first, and counteth the cost, whether he have sufficient to finish it."* (Luke 14:28) Without quality planning we are heading for a crash. One man said and I quote; *"aspire to acquire the desires you admire"*. Positive men and women are men/women of genuine impact in life. Life is full of warfare and not funfare.

----Meditation

Meditation is all it takes to remain positive in life. God is not mocked. Whatever we sow the same shall we reap. *David said "I have more understanding than all my teachers: for thy testimonies are my meditation."* (Psalm 119:99) Positive people do not panic in life. We must learn to be still in life. It is written *"Be still, and know that I am God: I will be exalted among the heathen, I will be exalted in the earth."* (Psalm 46:10).Most of the things we complain about are not worthy to complain about.

A brief biblical characters who developed positive attitude in their life time.

Daniel
In the face of hungry lions

"My God hath sent his angel, and hath shut the lions' mouths, that they have not hurt me: forasmuch as before him innocency was found in me; and also before thee, O king, have I done no hurt." **(Daniel 6:22)** Daniel was a man of positive attitude in His life time. Daniel was still in the face of hungry lions and survived the experience. You shall survive in the midst of roaring troubles in your life in the Name of Jesus.

Joseph
—from the pit into slavery

"Come, and let us sell him to the Ishmeelites, and let not our hand be upon him; for he is our brother and our flesh. And his brethren were content. Then there passed by Midianites merchantmen; and they drew and lifted up Joseph out of the pit, and sold Joseph to the Ishmeelites for twenty pieces of silver: and they brought Joseph into Egypt." **(Genesis 37:27-28)**

Joseph was a man of positive attitude in his life time. Although he was hated, and sold by his own brother, he was a young man who used positive attitude to overcome every prevailing challenge, he ever encountered in his lifetime.

----Apostle Paul

Apostle Paul was a great man of vigor. Despite all the oppositions confronting him, he was not only determined to be focused into his apostolic work, but also to die for it. In the scripture passage below, we understood that not even Agabus prophetic dream interpretation was enough to persuade him to succumb into fear.

"And when he was come unto us, he took Paul's girdle, and bound his own hands and feet, and said, Thus saith the Holy Ghost, So shall the Jews at Jerusalem bind the man that owneth this girdle, and shall deliver him into the hands of the Gentiles. And when we heard these things, both we, and they of that place, besought him not to go up to Jerusalem. Then Paul answered, What mean ye to weep and to break mine heart? for I am ready not to be bound only, but also to die at Jerusalem for the name of the Lord Jesus." (Acts 21:11-13)

Apostle Paul was a man of a positive attitude. That is why even when they thought that they had stoned him to death, he rose up and ran away to derbe. Apostle Paul was a positive man who was determined to do the will of our Father in Heaven. *"And there came thither certain Jews from Antioch and Iconium, who persuaded the people, and having stoned Paul, drew him out of the city, supposing he had been dead. Howbeit, as the disciples stood round about him, he rose up, and came into the city: and the next day he departed with Barnabas to Derbe."* **(Acts 14:19-20)**

CONDITION TO RECEIVE THE HOLY SPIRIT

~REPENTANCE

Repent, and be baptized every one of you in the name of Jesus Christ for the remission of sins, and ye shall receive the gift of the Holy Ghost.

~BE BAPTIZED

"….be baptized every one of you in the name of Jesus Christ for the remission of sins, and ye shall receive the gift of the Holy Ghost." (Acts 2:38)

~CONFESS OF YOUR SIN

"If we confess our sins, he is faithful and just to forgive us our sins, and to cleanse us from all unrighteousness." (1 John 1:9)

~ACKNOWLEDGMENT

"Acknowledge that you are a sinner and that Jesus Christ died for your sins." (Rom 3:23)

BORN AGAIN

"Jesus answered and said unto him, Verily, verily, I say unto thee, Except a man be born again, he cannot see the kingdom of God." (John 3:3)

CONDITIONS FOR THE ACQUINTANCE OF THE HOLY SPIRIT

WALKING IN THE SPIRIT:

"This I say then, Walk in the Spirit, and ye shall not fulfil the lust of the flesh."(Gal 5:17)

FAITH

"We having the same spirit of faith, according as it is written, I believed, and therefore have I spoken; we also believe, and therefore speak." (2 Cor 4:13)

WALK IN AGREEMENT

"Can two walk together, except they both agreed?" (Amos 3:3)

WALK IN LOVE

"And we have known and believed the love that God hath to us. God is love; and he that dwelleth in love dwelleth in God, and God in him." (1 John 4:16)

WALK IN TRUTH

"If the Son therefore shall make you free, ye shall be free indeed." (John 8:32)

DOMINATING PRAYER POINTS

I cancel my name and that of my family from the death register, with the fire of God, in the name of Jesus.

Every weapon of destruction fashioned against me and my family, be destroyed by the fire of God, in the name of Jesus

Power of God, fight for me in every area of my life, in Jesus' name.

Every hindrance to my breakthrough, be melted by the fire of God, in the name of Jesus.

Every evil power against me, be scattered by the thunder fire of God, in the name of Jesus.

Father Lord, destroy every evil man/woman in the name of Jesus.

Every failures of the past, be converted to success, in Jesus' name.

Father Lord, let the former rain, the latter rain and Your blessing pour down on me now.

Father Lord, let all the failure turn into success for me, in the name of Jesus.

Chapter 2   How To Remain Positive In Life

I receive power from on high and I paralyze all the powers of darkness that are diverting my blessings, in the name of Jesus.

Beginning from this day, I employ the services of the angels of God to open unto me every door of opportunity and breakthroughs, in the name of Jesus.

I will not go around in circles again, I will make progress, in the name of Jesus.

I shall not build for another to inhabit and I shall not plant for another to eat, in the name of Jesus.

I paralyse the powers of the emptier concerning my handywork, in the name of Jesus.

O Lord, let every locust, caterpillar and palmer-worm assigned to eat the fruit of my labour be roasted by the fire of God.

The enemy shall not spoil my testimony in this programme, in the name of Jesus.

By the blood of Jesus, I reject every backward journey, in the name of Jesus.

By the blood of Jesus, I paralyze every strongman attached to any area of my life, in the name of Jesus.

I pray, Let every agent of shame fashioned to work against my life be paralyzed, in the name of Jesus.

I paralyse the activities of household wickedness over my life, in the name of Jesus.

I quench every strange fire emanating from evil tongues against me, in the name of Jesus.

Father Lord, give me power for maximum achievement.

Heavenly father, give me comforting authority to achieve my goal.

Blood of Jesus Christ, defend and fortify me with Your power.

I paralyse every spirit of disobedience in my life, in Jesus' name.

I refuse to disobey the voice of God, in the name of Jesus.

Every root of rebellion in my life, be uprooted, in Jesus' name.

By the blood of Jesus, I destroy every witchcraft spirit in my life, in the name of Jesus.

Contradicting forces promoting hindrance in my life, die, in Jesus' name.

Chapter 2   How To Remain Positive In Life

Blood of Jesus, blot out every evil mark of witchcraft in my life, in the name of Jesus.

Every garment put upon me by witchcraft, be torn to pieces, in the name of Jesus.

Angels of God, begin to pursue my household enemies, let their ways be dark and slippery, in the name of Jesus.

Lord, confuse them and turn them against themselves.

By the blood of Jesus, I break every evil unconscious agreement with household enemies concerning my miracles, in the name of Jesus.

Household witchcraft, fall down and die, in the name of Jesus.

Father Lord, drag all the household wickedness to the Dead Sea and bury them there.

Father Lord, I reject to follow the evil pattern of remote control my household enemies.

My life, jump out from the cage of household wickedness, in the name of Jesus.

I command all my blessings and potentials buried by wicked household enemies to be exhumed, in the name of Jesus.

I will see the goodness of the Lord in the land of the living, in the name of Jesus.

Everything done against me to spoil my joy, receive destruction, in the name of Jesus.

Father Lord, as Abraham received favor in Your eyes, let me receive Your favor, so that I can excel in every area of my life.

Lord Jesus, help my shortcoming and infirmities in the name of Jesus.

It does not matter, whether I deserve it or not, I receive immeasurable favor from the Lord, in the name of Jesus.

By the blood of Jesus I receive every blessing God has apportioned to me in the name of Jesus.

My blessing will not be transferred to my neighbor in the name of Jesus.

Father Lord, disgrace every power that is tormenting my breakthrough in the name of Jesus.

Every step I take shall lead to outstanding success, in Jesus' name.

I shall prevail with man and with God in every area of my life, in the name of Jesus.

Chapter 2 — How To Remain Positive In Life

Every habitation of infirmity in my life, break to pieces, in the name of Jesus.

My body, soul and spirit, reject every evil load, in Jesus' name.

Evil foundation in my life, I pull you down today, in the mighty name of Jesus.

Every inherited sickness in my life, depart from me now, in the name of Jesus.

Every evil water in my body, get out, in the name of Jesus.

By the blood of Jesus, I cancel the effect of every evil dedication in my life, in the name of Jesus.

Holy Ghost fire, immunize my blood against satanic poisoning, in the name of Jesus.

Father Lord, put self control in my mouth, in the name of Jesus.

I refuse to get accustomed to sickness, in the name of Jesus.

Every door open to infirmity in my life, be permanently closed today, in the name of Jesus.

Every power contenting with God in my life, be roasted, in the name of Jesus.

Every power preventing God's glory from manifesting in my life, be paralysed, in the name of Jesus.

I loose myself from the spirit of desolation, in the name of Jesus.

Father Lord break me through in my home, in the name of Jesus.

Father Lord keep in me healthy, in the name of Jesus.

Father Lord break me through in my business, in the name of Jesus.

Let God be God in my economy, in the name of Jesus.

Glory of God, envelope every department of my life, in the name of Jesus.

The Lord that answereth by fire, be my God, in the name of Jesus.

By the blood of Jesus, all my enemies shall scatter to rise no more, in the name of Jesus.

Blood of Jesus, cry against all evil gatherings arranged for my sake, in the name of Jesus.

Father Lord, convert all my past failures to unlimited victories, in the name of Jesus.

Lord Jesus, create room for my advancement in every area of my life.

All evil thoughts against me, Lord turn them to be good for me.

Father Lord, give evil men for my life where evil decisions have been taken against me, in the name of Jesus.

Father Lord, advertise Your dumbfounding prosperity in my life.

Let the showers of dumbfounding prosperity fall in every department of my life, in the name of Jesus.

By the blood of Jesus, I claim all my prosperity in the name of Jesus.

Every door of my prosperity that has been shut, be opened now, in the name of Jesus.

Father Lord, convert my poverty to prosperity, in the name of Jesus.

Father Lord, convert my mistake to perfection, in the name of Jesus.

Father Lord, convert my frustration to fulfillment, in the name of Jesus.

Father Lord, bring honey out of the rock for me, in the name of Jesus.

By the blood of Jesus, I stand against every evil covenant of sudden death, in the name of Jesus.

By the blood of Jesus, I break every conscious and unconscious evil covenant of untimely death, in the name of Jesus.

You spirit of death and hell, you have no document in my life, in the name of Jesus.

You stones of death, depart from my ways, in the name of Jesus.

Father Lord, make me a voice of deliverance and blessing.

By the blood of Jesus, I tread upon the high places of the enemies, in the name of Jesus.

I bind and render useless, every blood sucking demon, in the name of Jesus.

You evil current of death, loose your grip over my life, in the name of Jesus.

By the blood of Jesus, I frustrate the decisions of the evil openers in my family, in the name of Jesus.

Chapter 2 — How To Remain Positive In Life

Fire of protection, cover my family, in the name of Jesus.

Father Lord, make my way perfect, in the name of Jesus.

Throughout the days of my life, I shall not be put to shame, in the name of Jesus.

By the blood of Jesus, I reject every garment of shame, in the name of Jesus.

By the blood of Jesus, I reject every shoe of shame, in the name of Jesus.

By the blood of Jesus, I reject every head-gear and cap of shame, in the name of Jesus.

Shamefulness shall not be my lot, in the name of Jesus.

Every demonic limitation of my progress as a result of shame, be removed, in the name of Jesus.

Every network of shame around me, be paralysed, in the name of Jesus.

Those who seek for my shame shall die for my sake, in the name of Jesus.

As far as shame is concerned, I shall not record any point for satan, in the name of Jesus.

I shall not eat the bread sorrow, shame, and defeat in Jesus Name.

No evil will touch me throughout my life, in the name of Jesus.

By the blood of Jesus, In every area of my life, my enemies will not catch me, in the name of Jesus.

By the blood of Jesus, In every area of my life, I shall run and not grow weary, I shall walk and shall not faint.

Father Lord, in every area of my life, let not my life disgrace You.

By the blood of Jesus, I will not be a victim of failure and I shall not bite my finger for any reason, in the name of Jesus.

Holy Spirit of God, Help me O Lord, to meet up with God's standard for my life.

By the blood of Jesus, I refuse to be a candidate to the spirit of amputation, in the name of Jesus.

By the blood of Jesus, with each day of my life, I shall move to higher ground, in the name of Jesus.

Every spirit of shame set in motion against my life, I bind you, in the name of Jesus.

Chapter 2   How To Remain Positive In Life

Every spirit competing with my breakthroughs, be chained, in the name of Jesus.

By the blood of Jesus, I bind every spirit of slavery , in the name of Jesus.

By the blood of Jesus, In every day of my life, I disgrace all my stubborn pursuers, in the name of Jesus.

By the blood of Jesus, I bind, every spirit of Herod, in the name of Jesus.

Every spirit challenging my God, be disgraced, in Jesus' name.

Every Red Sea before me, be parted, in the name of Jesus.

By the blood of Jesus, I command every spirit of bad ending to be bound in every area of my life, in the name of Jesus.

By the blood of Jesus, Every spirit of Saul, be disgraced in my life, in the name of Jesus.

By the blood of Jesus, Every spirit of Pharaoh, be disgraced in my life, in Jesus' name.

By the blood of Jesus, I reject every evil invitation to backwardness, in Jesus' name.

By the blood of Jesus, I command every stone of hindrance in my life to be rolled away, in the name of Jesus.

Father Lord, roll away every stone of poverty from my life, in the name Jesus.

Let every stone of infertility in my marriage be rolled away, in the name of Jesus.

Let every stone of non-achievement in my life be rolled away, in the name of Jesus.

My God, roll away every stone of hardship and slavery from my life, in the name of Jesus.

My God, roll away every stone of failure planted in my life, my home and in my business, in the name of Jesus.

You stones of hindrance, planted at the edge of my breakthroughs, be rolled away, in the name of Jesus.

You stones of stagnancy, stationed at the border of my life, be rolled away, in the name of Jesus.

Father Lord, I thank You for all the stones You have rolled away, I forbid their return, in the name of Jesus.

Let the power from above come upon me, in the name of Jesus.

Chapter 2   How To Remain Positive In Life

Father Lord, advertise Your power in every area of my life.

Father Lord, make me a power generator, throughout the days of my life, in the name of Jesus.

Let the power to live a holy life throughout the days of my life fall upon me, in the name of Jesus.

Let the power to live a victorious life throughout the days of my life fall upon me, in the name of Jesus.

Let the power to prosper throughout the days of my life fall upon me, in the name of Jesus.

Let the power to be in good health throughout the days of my life fall upon me, in the name of Jesus.

Let the power to disgrace my enemies throughout the days of my life fall upon me, in the name of Jesus.

Let the power of Christ rest upon me now, in the name of Jesus.

Let the power to bind and loose fall upon me now, in the name of Jesus.

Father Lord, let Your key of revival unlock every department of my life for Your revival fire, in the name of Jesus.

Every area of my life that is at the point of death, receive the touch of revival, in the name of Jesus.

Father Lord, send down Your fire and anointing into my life, in the name of Jesus.

Every uncrucified area in my life, receive the touch of fire and be crucified, in the name of Jesus.

Let the fire fall and consume all hindrances to my advancement, in the name of Jesus.

You stubborn problems in my life, receive the Holy Ghost dynamite, in the name of Jesus.

You carry-over miracle from my past, receive the touch of fire in the name of Jesus.

Holy Ghost fire, baptize me with prayer miracle, in Jesus' name.

By the blood of Jesus, Every area of my life that needs deliverance, receive the touch of fire and be delivered, in the name of Jesus.

Let my angels of blessing locate me now, in the name of Jesus.

Every satanic programme of impossibility, I cancel you now, in the name of Jesus.

Every household wickedness and its programme of impossibility, be paralysed, in the name of Jesus.

No curse will land on my head, in the name of Jesus.

Throughout the days of my life, I will not waste money on my health: the Lord shall be my healer, in the name of Jesus.

Throughout the days of my life, I will be in the right place at the right time.

Throughout the days of my life, I will not depart from the fire of God's protection, in the name of Jesus.

Throughout the days of my life, I will not be a candidate for incurable disease, in the name of Jesus.

Every weapon of captivity, be disgraced, in the name of Jesus.

Let every attack planned against the progress of my life be frustrated, in the name of Jesus.

I command the spirits of harassment and torment to leave me, in the name of Jesus.

Lord, begin to speak soundness into my mind and being.

I reverse every witchcraft curse issued against my progress.

I condemn all the spirits condemning me, in the name of Jesus.

Let divine accuracy come into my life and operations, in the name of Jesus.

No evil directive will manifest in my life, in the name of Jesus.

Let the plans and purposes of heaven be fulfilled in my life, in the name of Jesus.

O Lord, bring to me friends that reverence Your name and keep all others away.

Let divine strength come into my life, in the name of Jesus.

Let every stronghold working against my peace be destroyed, in the name of Jesus.

Let the power to destroy every decree of darkness operating in my life fall upon me now, in the name of Jesus.

Lord, deliver my tongue from evil silence.

Lord, let my tongue tell others of Your life.

Lord, loose my tongue and use it for Your glory.

Lord, let my tongue bring straying sheep back to the fold.

Lord, let my tongue strengthen those who are discouraged.

Lord, let my tongue guide the sad and the lonely.

Lord, baptise my tongue with love and fire.

Let every unrepentant and stubborn pursuers be disgraced in my life, in the name of Jesus.

Let every iron-like curse working against my life be broken by the blood of Jesus, in the name of Jesus.

Let every problem designed to disgrace me receive open shame, in the name of Jesus.

Let every problem anchor in my life be uprooted, in Jesus' name.

Multiple evil covenants, be broken by the blood of Jesus, in the name of Jesus.

Multiple curses, be broken by the blood of Jesus, in Jesus' name.

Everything done against me with evil padlocks, be nullified by the blood of Jesus, in the name of Jesus.

Everything done against me at any cross-roads, be nullified by the blood of Jesus, in the name of Jesus.

Let every stubborn and prayer resisting demon receive stones of fire and thunder, in the name of Jesus.

Every stubborn and prayer resisting sickness, loose your evil hold upon my life, in the name of Jesus.

Every problem associated with the dead, be smashed by the blood of Jesus, in the name of Jesus.

I recover my stolen property seven fold, in the name of Jesus.

Let every evil memory about me be erased by the blood of Jesus, in the name of Jesus.

By the blood of Jesus, I disallow my breakthroughs from being caged, in Jesus' name.

Let the sun of my prosperity arise and scatter every cloud of poverty, in the name of Jesus.

I decree unstoppable advancement upon my life, in Jesus' name.

I soak every day of my life in the blood of Jesus and in signs and wonders, in the name of Jesus.

I break every stronghold of oppression in my life.

Let every satanic joy about my life be terminated, in the name of Jesus.

I paralyze every household wickedness, in the name of Jesus.

Let every satanic spreading river dry up by the blood of Jesus, in the name of Jesus.

I bind every ancestral spirit and command them to loose their hold over my life, in the name of Jesus.

WISDOM KEYS

— Every Productive Society is a society heading to the top.

— Millions of Nigerians run away from Nigeria, very few Nigerians stay in Nigeria.

— My decision to return Nigeria is the will of God for my life

— My short coming in America after 18 years, trained me to be wise, to think, reflect and reason appropriately.

— If you train your mind to reason it will train your hands to earn money.

— It is absurd to use the money of the heathen to build the kingdom of the living God.

— Every Ministry reveals its agenda and goal either at the beginning or at the end. Be careful of your life it is your first Ministry.

— The average American mind is conditioned for a continual quest to get new things and (discard the former) and throw away old things.

— When I considered well, my BMW jeep became my initial deposit for the work of the ministry in Nigeria.

— Money will never fall from any tree.

— Department or person. Make up your mind to be independent today.

— Everyone is waiting for you to change your mind until you change your thinking nothing changes around you.

— Multiple academic degrees in other discipline gave me the chance to think, reflect and reason

— What so everyone are thinking and reflecting at the moment reveals you to the time and the now factor

— All events and intents are the product of precise thought processes, accurate reason every event is designed for a designated timeline

— Wisdom is your ability to think, to create and invent. If you can think wise enough you will come out of penury

— The distance between you and success is your creative ability to think reason and reflect accurate.

— Success is the result of hard work, commitment resolve and determination learning from past mistakes and failing.

— If you organize your mind you have organized your life and destiny.

— There is a thin line between success and failure. If you look above and beyond you are on your way to success.

— Wealth is your ability to think, power is your ability to reason and success is your ability to be informed.

— If you can make use of your mind by thinking and reasoning God will make use of your life and destiny.

— Think and Be Great.

— Reflect, Reason, think and be great.

— Famous people are born of woman

— That you will make it is your intention; that you will survive is your resolve, that you will succeed with changes is your determination, personal efforts and hard work.

— No man was born a failure. Lack of vision is the end product of failure.

— Working with mental patients encourages and aspire me to be a productive observant and dedicated to my assignment.

— Successful people are not magicians, it is the will power combined with hard work, and determination and a resolve to succeed that make them succeed.

Chapter 2   How To Remain Positive In Life

— In the unequivocal state of the mind, intention is not a location or a position it is the state of the mind.

— So many people think, that they think. The mind is used to think, reflect, and reason. You will remain blind with your eye open until you can see with your mind by thinking.

— There is no favoritism in accurate and precise calculation.

— Although knowledge is power, information is the key and gateway to a great future.

— It will take the hand of God to move the hand of man.

— With the backing of the great wise God, nothing will disconnect you from your inheritance.

— As long as you have wisdom and understanding of God, Satan and evil cannot manipulate your life and destiny.

— You have come this far by yourself judgment and decision you have made in the past, now lean and listen to God for another dimension of greatness.

— Great people are common people it is extra ordinary effort and the price of sacrifice that produces greatness.

— As a mental direct care worker I saw a great pastor and a motivational speaker within myself.

— Menial job does not reduce your self-worth, until you resolve to achieve greatness see greatness in all you do; you will never count in your community.

— The principle of Jesus will solve your gambling and addiction problems

— The man of Jesus will lead you into heaven,

— Everyone have their self-appraisal and what they think about you. Until you discover yourself other opinion about you will alter the real you.

— Supervisors and directors are just a position in the chain of command in a work place. Never allow your supervisor hierarchy to alter your opinion about yourself.

— Everyone can come out of debt if they make up their mind.

— That I am not a decision maker at work does not diminish my contribution to my world.

— Although it appears like it was a poor decision to accept a direct care employment at a psychiatric hospital as I reflect of my nine years of experience, it became apparent that I have learnt and experienced enough for my next assignment in life.

Chapter 2   How To Remain Positive In Life

— Self-encouragement and determination is a resolve of the heart.

— If you are determined to make a difference, and do the things that make a difference you will eventually make a difference.

— Good things do not come easy

— Short cuts will cut your life short.

— Those who look ahead move ahead.

— Life is all about making an impact. In your life time strive to make an impact in your community.

— Make friends and connect with people who are moving ahead of you in life.

— If you can look around well you have come a long way in your life, made a lot of difference and realized a lot of success in life.

— If you are my old friend, hurry up to reach out to me before I become a stranger to you.

— Everything I am blessed with inspirations from God, that change my definition and interpretation of the world around me.

— I thought I was stagnant and lonely until I looked around and noticed my children running around and my wife cooking.

— At 40 I resigned my Job to seek the Lord forever.

— My ministry took a drastic rise to the top when the wisdom of God visited me with knowledge and understanding.

— You will be a better person, if you understand the characteristics of your personality – your mood swings, attitudes, and habits.

— It is the seed of love you sow into the heart of a child and a woman that you reap in due time.

— Love is not selfish, love share everything including the concealed secrets of the mind.

— As long as you have a prayer life and a bible; you will never feel lonely, rejected, and idle in the race of life.

— When good friends disconnect from you, let them go, they might have seen something new in a different direction.

— Confidence in yourself and in God is the only way to bring you out of captivity.

Chapter 2   How To Remain Positive In Life

— Never train a child to waste his/her time.

— The mind is the greatest assets of a great future.

— You walk by common sense run by principles and fly by instruction.

— Those who fly in flight of life fly alone.

— Up in the air you are alone. No one can toll you accept the compass of knowledge and information.

— I have seen a towing vehicle I have seen a towing ship I have never seen a tolling airplane.

— I exercise my judgment and make a decision every minute of the day.

— Decisions are crucial, critical and vital with reference to your future.

— So many people wish for a great future. You can only work towards a great future.

— Your celebrity status began when you discovered your talent. What are you good at? Work at it with all commitment.

— Prayers will sustain you but the wisdom of God will prosper you.

— When I met Oyedepo, his teachings changed my perspective. But when I met Ibiyeomie; His teaching changed my perception.

— I will be successful in ministry if only I concentrate and focus my energy in the work of the ministry.

— It took the late Dr. Vincent Pearle Norman's book to open my mind towards kingdom success.

CHAPTER 3

PRAYER OF SALVATION

"Neither is there salvation in any other: for there is none other name under heaven given among men, whereby we must be saved."
Acts 4:12

The purpose of this book is to spread the word of God in print. The purpose is defeated if you do not accept the Lord as your personal savior and Lord over your life.

What must I do to determine my divine visitation?

To determine divine visitation you must be born again! The word says, *"As many as received him, to them gave He power to become the sons of God. Even to them that believe on his name."* (John 1:12)

To qualify for divine visitation, do the following with sincerity—

1) Acknowledge that you are a sinner and that He died for you. (Romans 3:23)

2) Repent of your sins. (Acts 3:19, Luke 13:5, 2 Peter 3:9)

3) Believe in your heart that Jesus died for your sin. (Romans 10:10)

4) Confess Jesus as the Lord over your life. (Romans 10:10, Acts 2:21)

"Therefore if any man be in Christ, he is a new creature: old things are passed away; behold, all things are become new." (2 Cor 5:17)

Now repeat this Prayer after me

Say Lord Jesus, I accept you today, as my Lord and my savior, forgive me of my sins wash me with your blood. Right now, I believe, I am sanctified, I am save, I am free, I am free from the Power of sin to serve the Lord Jesus. Thank you Lord for saving me. Amen.

Congratulations: You are now...

A BORN AGAIN CHRISTIAN.

Again I say to you—

CONGRATULATIONS!

I guarantee you! Watch the Spirit of God bear witness with your Spirit confirming His word with signs following. The word says, *"The Spirit itself beareth witness with our spirit, that we are the children of God."* (Romans 8:16)

Join a bible believing church or join us on our weekly and Sunday worship services at 343 Sanford Avenue, Newark, New Jersey 07106.

MIRACLE CARE OUTREACH

*"...But that the members should have
the same care one for another"*
1 Corinthians 12:25

We are all members of the body of Christ. Jesus commanded us to love our neighbor as ourselves. This includes caring for one another as a member of one body. True love is expressed in caring and giving. The word says for God so Love He gave….

Reach out to someone in need of Jesus, help someone in crisis find Christ. Look out and prove your love to Jesus by caring and inviting your friends and associates to find Jesus the Healer.

Invite your friends to our Home Care Cell Fellowship (Miracle chapel Intl Satellite fellowship) In the USA at 33 Schley Street Newark New Jersey 07112. Home Care Cell fellowship Group meets every Tuesday at 6:00pm-7:00pm.

If you are in Nigeria—**MIRACLE OF GOD MINISTRIES**, aka **"MIRACLE CHAPEL INTL"** Mpama –Egbu-Owerri Imo state Nigeria.

Chapter 3   Prayer of Salvation

LIFE IS NOT ALL ABOUT DURATION— BUT ITS ALL ABOUT DONATION

What does the above statement mean?….

Life consists not in accumulation of material wealth. (Luke 12:15) But it's all about liberality…i.e., what you can give and share with others. (Proverbs 11:25) When you live for others, you live forever—because you out-live your generation by the legacy you live behind after you depart into glory to be with the Lord. But when you live to yourself, when you are reduced to SELF—you are easily forgotten when you die and depart in glory.

Permit me to admonish you today to live your life to be a blessing to a soul connected to you today. I want you to know that so many souls are connected and looking up to you, and through you so many souls will be saved and rescued from destruction. Will you disciple someone today to find Jesus Christ?

As a genuine Christian; it is your duty to evangelize Jesus Christ to all you meet on your way. Jesus is still in the healing business—Jesus is still doing miracles from time of old to now. Therefore, tell someone about Jesus Christ today, disciple and bring them to Church. *Philip findeth Nathanael...* (John 1:45)

Please to prove the sincerity of your love for God today; please become a soul winner. The dignity of your Christianity is hidden in your boldness to proclaim and evangelize Jesus Christ to all you meet on your way. There is a question mark on the integrity of your Christianity until you become a life soul winner. Invite someone to join us worship the Lord Jesus this coming Sunday. Amen

Chapter 3   Prayer of Salvation

MIRACLE OF GOD MINISTRIES

PILLARS OF THE COMMISSION

We Believe Preach and Practice the following:

1) We believe and preach Salvation to every living human being

2) We believe and preach Repentance and forgiveness of sins

3) We believe and preach the baptism of the Holy Spirit and Spiritual gifts

4) We believe and teach the Prosperity

5) We believe and preach Divine Healing and Miracles (Signs &Wonder)

6) We believe and preach Faith

7) We believe and proclaim the Power of God (Supernatural)

8) We believe and proclaim Praise& Worship to God

9) We believe and preach Wisdom

10) We believe and preach Holiness (Consecration)

11) We believe and preach Vision

12) We believe and teach the Word of God

13) We believe and teach Success

14) We believe and practice Prayer

15) We believe and teach Deliverance

These 15 stones form the Pillars of Our Commission. Become part of this church family and follow this great move of God.

MY HEART FELT PRAYER FOR YOU

It is my prayer that you testify today about the goodness of the Lord. I desire for you to have an encounter with our Lord Jesus Christ.

Now let me Pray for you:

Father Lord, I pray and crave for the Holy Spirit, to rekindle the life of this precious love one. In the Name of Jesus. I pray we develop a positive attitude in life against all obstacles facing us in the Name of Jesus. Amen

Chapter 3   Prayer of Salvation

CONCLUSION

"And she said, Let thine handmaid find grace in thy sight. So the woman went her way, and did eat, and her countenance was no more sad.
(1 Samuel 1:18)

Although repentance is the key into deliverance and promotion in life. Unless you change the way you think, you cannot change the outcome of your life. For every one that desired to encounter testimonies in life, we must change the way we think in our heart, confess the Lord Jesus, and forsake our sinful ways.

"Let us hear the conclusion of the whole matter: Fear God, and keep his commandments: for this is the whole duty of man. For God shall bring every work into judgment, with every secret thing, whether it be good, or whether it be evil."
(Eccl1 2:13-14)

The book will remain a story to anyone who is not ready to make a decision for Jesus Christ. One man said if you failed to plan you have planned to fail in life. We want you to make plans to make heaven. The bible says *"For God shall bring every work into judgment, with every secret thing, whether it be good, or whether it be evil."* (Eccl12:14) If you are a born again Christian; we like to encourage you in your Christian life. If you are not a born again Christian we can help you here receive genuine salvation.

What must I do to determine my divine visitation?

To determine divine visitation you must be born again! The word says, *"As many as received him, to them gave He power to become the sons of God. Even to them that believe on his name."* (John 1:12)

To qualify for divine visitation, do the following with sincerity—

1) Acknowledge that you are a sinner and that He died for you. (Romans 3:23)

2) Repent of your sins. (Acts 3:19, Luke 13:5, 2 Peter 3:9)

3) Believe in your heart that Jesus died for your sin. (Romans 10:10)

4) Confess Jesus as the Lord over your life. (Romans 10:10, Acts 2:21)

"Therefore if any man be in Christ, he is a new creature: old things are passed away; behold, all things are become new." (2 Cor 5:17)

Chapter 3   Prayer of Salvation

Now repeat this Prayer after me

Say Lord Jesus, I accept you today, as my Lord and my savior, forgive me of my sins wash me with your blood. Right now, I believe, I am sanctified, I am save, I am free, I am free from the Power of sin to serve the Lord Jesus. Thank you Lord for saving me. Amen.

Congratulations: You are now...

A BORN AGAIN CHRISTIAN.

Again I say to you—

CONGRATULATIONS!

I guarantee you! Watch the Spirit of God bear witness with your Spirit confirming His word with signs following. The word says, *"The Spirit itself beareth witness with our spirit, that we are the children of God."* (Romans 8:16)

Join a bible believing church or join us on our weekly and Sunday worship services at 343 Sanford Avenue, Newark, New Jersey 07106.

ITS TIME TO TURN TO GOD IN PRAYER AND IN THANKSGIVING

Unless we turn to God in prayers and in intercession, we will miss our glorious future in life. God is the source of life. If we must align with divine plan we must turn to God in prayer and in thanksgiving in life. We must not miss our greatest opportunity of salvation in life.

It is written *"If my people, which are called by my name, shall humble themselves, and pray, and seek my face, and turn from their wicked ways; then will I hear from heaven, and will forgive their sin, and will heal their land."* **(2 Chronicle 7:14)**

We are told *"Woe unto him that striveth with his Maker! Let the potsherd strive with the potsherds of the earth. Shall the clay say to him that fashioneth it, What makest thou? or thy work, He hath no hands?"* **(Isaiah 45:9)**

We must return to God with a genuine heart, for our deliverance, breakthrough, and supernatural promotion in every aspect of our lives. If there are any prevailing challenges against our life, *I pray in the Name of Jesus, let the power of God subdue the wicked one against your life even now in the Mighty Name of Jesus. Amen.* Remember, you can always take advantage of our prayer hotline. For all spiritual emergency please call 973-393-8518.

CHAPTER 4

ABOUT THE AUTHOR

Rev Franklin N Abazie is the founding and Presiding Pastor of Miracle of God Ministries with headquarters in Newark, New Jersey USA and a branch church in Owerri- Imo State Nigeria. He is following the footsteps of one of his mentors, Oral Roberts (Healing Evangelist) of the blessed memory. The Lord passed Oral Roberts healing mantle two days before he went to be with the Lord at age 91 into the hand of healing evangelist-Rev Franklin N Abazie in a vision.

In all his services the Power and Presence of God is present to heal all in his audience. He is an ordained man of God with a Healing Ministry reviving the healing and miracle ministry of Jesus Christ of Nazareth.

Pastor Franklin N Abazie, is called by God with a unique mandate: **"THE MOMENT IS DUE TO IMPACT YOUR WORLD THROUGH THE REVIVAL OF THE HEALING & MIRACLE MINISTRY OF JESUS CHRIST OF NAZARETH**

"I AM SENDING YOU TO RESTORE HEALTH UNTO THEE AND I WILL HEAL THEE OF THY WOUNDS. SAID THE LORD OF HOST"

Rev. Abazie is a gifted ardent Teacher of the word of God who operates also in the office of a Prophet, generating and attracting undeniable signs & wonders, special miracles and healings, with apostolic fireworks of the Holy Ghost. He is the founding and presiding senior Pastor of this fast growing Healing ministry. He has written over 86 inspirational, healing and transforming books covering almost all aspect of divine healing and life. He is happily married and blessed with children.

Chapter 4   About The Author

BOOKS BY REV FRANKLIN N ABAZIE

1) The Outcome of Faith
2) Understanding the secret of prevailing Prayers
3) Commanding Abundance
4) Understanding the secret of the man God uses
5) Activating my due Season
6) Overcoming Divine Verdicts
7) The Outcome of Divine Wisdom
8) Understanding God's Restoration Mandate
9) Walking in the Victory and Authority of the truth
10) Gods Covenant Exemption
11) Destiny Restoration Pillars
12) Provoking Acceptable Praise
13) Understanding Divine Judgment
14) Activating Angelic Re-enforcement
15) Provoking Un-Merited Favor
16) The Benefits of the Speaking faith
17) Understanding Divine Arrangement
18) Put your faith to work
19) Developing a positive attitude in life
20) The Power of Prevailing faith
21) Inexplicable faith
22) The intellectual components of Redemption.
23) Dominating Controlling Spirit
24) Understanding Divine Prosperity
25) Understanding the secret of the man God Uses
26) Retaining Your Inheritance
27) Never give up hope
28) Commanding Angelic Escorts
29) The winner's faith
30) Understanding Your Guardian Angels
31) Overcoming the Dominion of Sin
32) Understanding the Voice of God
33) The Outstanding benefits of the Anointing

34) The Audacity of the Blood of Jesus
35) Walking in the Reality of the Anointing
36) The Mystery of Divine supply
37) Understanding Your Harvest Season
38) Activating Your Success Buttons
39) Overcoming the forces of Darkness
40) Overcoming the devices of the devil
41) Overcoming Demonic agents
42) Overcoming the sorrows of failure
43) Rejecting the Sorrows of failure
44) Resisting the Sorrows of Poverty
45) The Restoring broken Marriages.
46) Redeeming Your Days
47) The force of Vision
48) Overcoming the forces of ignorance
49) Understanding the sacrifice of small beginning
50) The might of small beginning
51) Praying in the Spirit
52) Dominating controlling Spirits
53) Breaking the shackles of the curse of the law
54) Covenant keys to answered prayers
55) Wisdom for Signs & Wonders
56) Wisdom for generational Impact
57) Wisdom for Marriage Stability
58) Understanding the number of your Days
59) Enforcing Your Kingdom Rights
60) Escaping the traps of immoralities
61) Escaping the trap of Poverty
62) Accessing Biblical Prosperity
63) Accessing True Riches in Christ
64) Silencing the Voice of the Accuser
65) Overcoming the forces of oppositions
66) Quenching the voice of the avenger
67) Silencing demonic Prediction & Projection
68) Silencing Your Mocker
69) Understanding the Power of the Holy Ghost

Chapter 4   About The Author

70) Understanding the baptism of Power
71) The Mystery of the Blood of Jesus
72) Understanding the Mystery of Sanctification
73) Understanding the Power of Holiness
74) Praying in the spirit
75) Activating the Forces of Vengeance
76) Appreciating the Mystery of Restoration
77) Covenant Keys to Answered Prayers
78) Engaging the mystery of the blood
79) Commanding the Power of the Speaking faith
80) Uprooting the forces against Your Rising
81) Overcoming mere success syndrome
82) Understanding Divine Sentence
83) Understanding the Mystery of Praise
84) Understanding the Author of Faith
85) The Mystery of the finisher of faith
86) Where is your trust?

MIRACLE OF GOD MINISTRIES

*NIGERIA CRUSADE
2012*

MIRACLE OF GOD MINISTRIES

*NIGERIA CRUSADE
2012*

MIRACLE OF GOD MINISTRIES

NIGERIA CRUSADE 2012

www.ingramcontent.com/pod-product-compliance
Lightning Source LLC
Chambersburg PA
CBHW071751080526
44588CB00013B/2210